true love PROJECT

CLAYTON & SHARIE KING

LifeWay Press®
Nashville, Tennessee

ISBN: 978-1-4158-7829-3
Item: 005558779

Dewey Decimal Classification Number: 306.73
Subject Headings: CHRISTIAN LIFE \ SEXUAL ABSTINENCE \ GOSPEL

Printed in the United States of America

Student Ministry Publishing
LifeWay Church Resources
One LifeWay Plaza
Nashville, TN 37234-0144

We believe that the Bible has God for its author; salvation for its end; and truth, without any mixture of error, for its matter
and that all Scripture is totally true and trustworthy.
To review LifeWay's doctrinal guideline, please visit *www.lifeway.com/doctrinalguideline.*

All Scripture quotations are taken from the Holman Christian Standard Bible © 1999, 2000, 2002, 2003, 2009 by Holman
Bible Publishers.
Used by permission.

table of contents

about the authors

CLAYTON KING is President of Crossroads Ministries, the Teaching Pastor at Newspring Church, and Campus Pastor at Liberty University. He is an evangelist, author, and missionary. Clayton began preaching at the age of 14 and has traveled to 36 countries and 46 states. He's written nine books and preached to over three million people. Clayton is passionate about seeing people far from God repent of their sin and begin a relationship with Jesus. He loves to pastor pastors and empower Christians for ministry. He also loves four-wheelers, action figures, black coffee, and his wife and two sons. For more information about Clayton and his ministries, visit him at claytonking.com and crossroadsworldwide.com

SHARIE KING was saved at the age of 11 and sensed God calling her to share her story of rescue and redemption. She has shared the gospel at Crossroads camps, college campuses, and mission trips in countries like Poland, India, and Malaysia. Sharie speaks at women's events in local churches and conferences across America, teaching on marriage and ministry with her husband, Clayton. She also speaks on sexual purity, finding your identity in Christ, and overcoming fear. Sharie has a heart to see women embrace the truth of the gospel. She loves painting, writing, and homeschooling her two boys. For more about Sharie, visit her at sharieking.com

1

session 1:
GOD'S STORY, YOUR STORY

This study isn't primarily about issues related to sex, purity, and romance. Primarily, it is about helping you understand those things in light of God's eternal, bigger story. Only when you are able to see your role in that story will you know what God wants to do with you and through you.

1 session 1: GOD'S STORY, YOUR STORY

This may sound strange, but we are going to begin our study on purity, sex, and romance by not talking about purity, sex, or romance. There's no doubt that the things we talk about in this lesson are directly related to issues of physical intimacy, but in order to correctly tackle the issues surrounding sex and purity, it is essential that we first begin with the One who created these things. By understanding God's story, we will gain a better understanding of ourselves and how our individual stories fit into His larger story.

video guide:

CREATION

God made us because He _____ to.

You were fashioned and designed to _____ like God.

FALL

We see in Adam and Eve a reflection of our own _____. We think we know better than _____.

We believe He is _____ something from us that would make us happier.

REDEMPTION

The word that best describes this process of being rescued from sin and destruction is
" _____."

In essence, it refers to the fact that Jesus _____ the perfect life we could never _____.

RESTORATION

Part of this restoration means He wants to _____ us to the place He originally intended us to be.

Restoration touches every part of your life, repairing your perspective on _____ and _____.

video feedback:

+ Why would it be important to begin a study on purity and sex with a discussion about God's story?

+ What does Clayton mean when he talks about understanding your individual story in light of God's bigger story?

+ How does each of the story elements (creation, fall, redemption, restoration) speak directly to issues of relationships, sexuality, purity, etc.?

CREATION:

FALL:

REDEMPTION:

RESTORATION:

+ What do these story elements communicate about God's character and intention for people?

Develop and post a personal tweet or Facebook status related to this session using the hashtag #trueloveproject

part 1: CREATION

Share your favorite stories in the categories below.

Favorite story in a book:

Favorite story in a movie/television series:

Favorite personal story:

Everyone loves a good story. The reason we connect so deeply with stories is because we are all part of a much bigger, more important story that has been playing out since the dawn of human history. It's a story written by God Himself. He is the main character, and His son, Jesus, is the hero. We are a part of the cast of characters and the plot revolves around a pretty big problem—a universal resistance to God and His ways.

Do you consider yourself a character is God's story? Why or why not? How can knowing that you are a part of God's bigger story bring meaning and fulfillment to your life?

Act One of God's story began long ago.

> *Then God said, "Let Us make man in Our image, according to Our likeness. They will rule the fish of the sea, the birds of the sky, the livestock, all the earth, and the creatures that crawl on the earth." So God created man in His own image; He created him in the image of God; He created them male and female. God blessed them, and God said to them, "Be fruitful, multiply, fill the earth, and subdue it."*
>
> (GEN. 1:26-28A)

+ Why is it important to emphasize how humanity came into existence?

+ Why is being created in God's image an important part of your identity? Is there any use in finding your identity in anything other than the image of God? Why or why not?

Our identity should be wrapped up in being image-bearers of Christ. God's original blueprint was that we look like Him, reflecting His relationship within the Trinity (Father, Son, Spirit) as we love one another in friendships and marriage.

part 2: FALL

In the midst of this perfect environment filled with life, wonder, work, and pleasure, God graciously allowed Adam and Eve to enjoy all of the good gifts that grew in the garden of Eden. There was, however, one item that God banned—fruit from "the tree of the knowledge of good and evil." God lovingly warned them against eating from the tree, saying, "…the day you eat from it, you will certainly die." (See Gen. 2:16-17.)

✝ Genesis 3 marks the beginning of Act Two in God's grand story. **Read Genesis 3:1-19**, and summarize what happened in the garden of Eden.

Every story has a main villain. In Genesis 3, we meet the villain of this story—the serpant. He goes by several names: Satan, Lucifer, the Devil, the Accuser, and the Evil One. He hates God, and he hates us because we were made in God's image.

✝ **Read John 10:10 and 1 Peter 5:8.** What is Satan's desire?

✝ While it's Satan's desire to steal, kill, and destroy, what has God done to save us from destruction? **Read Romans 5:6-11.**

This is where the story takes a dramatic turn. Adam and Eve were deceived and they disobeyed. They rebelled against the God who made them and gave them all good things. They took the fruit and ate it, believing that they could be like God. Immediately, their eyes were opened—but not to greater pleasure and happiness. The serpent had lied. They saw their shame, nakedness, and sin. Adam and Eve were embarrassed, so they tried to hide from God.

part 3: REDEMPTION

Without the fall, there would be no need for Act Three in God's story—the story of redemption. It is here where we see resolution take place. It is the "happy ending" of this unfolding drama.

+ What was so bad about the fall? Answer this question based on the verses below:

ROMANS 5:12

ROMANS 6:23

EPHESIANS 2:1-3

These verses show that the relationship between humanity and God had been broken, making us desperate for a reconciled relationship with Him. Just when we thought that there was no possible way things could get better, God crashed into the middle of the problem to rescue us from sin and destruction through His Son, Jesus Christ. He redeemed us.

+ Explain *redemption* based upon the following verses:

EPHESIANS 1:6-8

COLOSSIANS 1:13-15

HEBREWS 9:14-16

+ Why do you think that redemption is a common theme in most stories? Why would a story seem to be incomplete without it?

part 4: RESTORATION

You may think that redemption marks the end of the story, but you would be wrong. God's intent is not just to spare us from hell; He has a much bigger plan for all of His creation. He never gave up on the world that He started in Eden. He wants to restore us to the place He originally intended us to be—with Him, in loving fellowship, living together in a world created to sustain life and joy.

+ Revelation 21:1-3 paints a picture of future restoration. Summarize this passage below.

Complete restoration will occur in the future when Jesus returns to put a final end to sin and death. However, restoration is also available right now because of Jesus' redemption. If you belong to Jesus, He is already doing a work of restoration in you.

+ How has Jesus changed parts of your life to reflect more of Him?

+ When you recognize Jesus as Lord, you will grow more and more like Him. How will this change the way you view sexuality?

Restoration will touch every part of your life, including your perspective on love and relationships. Remember that God began creation with a man and a woman who reflected the image of God together. While the fall altered God's perfect design, Jesus stepped in to restore all things. His presence will change how you see your sexuality, your desires, your body, and your craving for attention. He has the power to transform your expectations about relationships, showing you how to serve and sacrifice for the person you love. His restoration means that you don't let sexual cravings, emotional loneliness, or past mistakes control you. Instead, you are controlled by the Holy Spirit who is living and working in you.

session 1: GOD'S STORY, YOUR STORY

+ Notes on interview with Mark Batterson:

CONSIDER THIS

+ Why is it important to begin this study by focusing on God rather than on the topic at hand?

+ Why do the topics of sex and purity make more sense in the context of God's larger story? Why is it important to know that our lives are part of something much bigger than ourselves?

+ What is the difference between the third and fourth act of God's story?

HIGHLIGHTS

From Clayton's teaching, your personal reflection, and the interview, what impacted you from this session?

+

+

+

ACTION POINTS

+

+

+

session 2
THE COST OF OWNERSHIP

"Before you can understand love, you must understand lordship. Before you decide who you will love, you must decide who is your Lord."

-CLAYTON KING

2 session 2: THE COST OF OWNERSHIP

As we learned in the first session, we are all part of God's redemptive story. We are being remade as we experience redemption through His Son. In this session, we will discover that the main character in God's story is His Son, Jesus. Because of who Jesus is, we should submit to His lordship over our lives and recognize that He knows best when it comes to issues of sex and purity.

video guide:

Every single important thing in your life revolves around one issue, and that is the issue of _____.

Whoever has the title of _____ in your life is the ultimate ruler and calls all the shots.

FOLLOW HIS LORDSHIP:

When Jesus is Lord, you recognize the _____ He made when He died in your place to reconcile you to God.

When Jesus is Lord, you want to honor His _____ in your relationships and live by His _____ that govern your body and sexual desires.

When you are lord, you're _____ primarily by whatever it is that you _____ at any given moment.

If you are the lord of your life, then you are the ultimate _____ and you become a _____ unto yourself.

RECOGNIZE THAT HE KNOWS BEST WHEN IT COMES TO SEX AND PURITY:

Because He _____ about you and because He _____ best (and can see the consequences of your sins and bad decisions), He _____ you to give control of your life to Him.

Before you can understand _____, you must understand _____.

Before you decide who you will _____, you must decide who is your _____.

video feedback:

+ Summarize what it means for Jesus to be Lord over your life. What are the implications in the areas of romance and intimacy?

+ What signs might indicate that you are lord over your life? What signs might indicate that Jesus is Lord over your life?

+ Why is trying to be lord over your life detrimental to your health? Why is it actually good and joyful to have Jesus be your Lord?

+ How was C.S. Lewis' story about children playing near the edge of the cliff helpful in thinking about how God relates to His children? Do you believe that God is working for your good and joy? Why or why not?

Develop and post a personal tweet or Facebook status related to this session using the hashtag #trueloveproject

part 1: LORDSHIP REQUIRED

What does the concept of lordship mean to you? Start by imagining someone that is more powerful than the president, more influential than a prime minister, and more prominent than a king or queen—but don't stop there. Now imagine this power on a universal scale that includes our world plus all other planets, solar systems, universes—the entirety of the infinite cosmos! You've now begun to get a glimpse into the concept of lordship.

+ What are some additional examples that illustrate the concept of lordship?

After speaking at a public school assembly years ago, a very upset 16-year-old girl approached me. She said, "Who do you think you are? You can't tell me who I can sleep with or what I can do with my boyfriend, or my girlfriend, or even a perfect stranger I meet at a party. It's my body and I will do what I want with it!"

+ If Jesus is Lord over all things, how does that change the way we view our bodies? How does 1 Corinthians 6:9-11 help answer this?

+ When Jesus is your Savior, He is also the Lord of your life. What does Romans 10:9 have to say about the connection between lordship and personal salvation?

+ If Jesus is our Lord, why are we not free to enjoy sex apart from His design?

+ Why would Jesus' lordship in our lives lead to greater fulfillment in the areas of romance and intimacy?

The job of ruler, boss, and master needs to be filled by someone who is smart and experienced enough to see things that you don't see and to know things that you couldn't possibly know. You need a boss that can handle the job.

part 2: THE EXTENT OF LORDSHIP

When you declare Jesus to be Lord of your life, He then gets to call all the shots.

✝ How does Jesus call the shots in the following areas of your life?

Who you date:

What you watch on TV/Internet:

What you desire:

What you fantasize about:

> He is the image of the invisible God, the firstborn over all creation.
> For everything was created by Him, in heaven and on earth,
> the visible and the invisible, whether thrones or dominions
> or rulers or authorities—all things have been created through Him and for Him.
> He is before all things, and by Him all things hold together.
> He is also the head of the body, the church;
> He is the beginning, the firstborn from the dead,
> so that He might come to have first place in everything.
> For God was pleased to have all His fullness dwell in Him,
> and through Him to reconcile everything to Himself
> by making peace through the blood of His cross,—
> whether things on earth or things in heaven.
>
> (COL. 1:15-20)

✝ How does this passage relate to the lordship of Christ over all things, including sexual intimacy?

Settling the issue of lordship is foundational to your life, not only for the pursuit of purity, but also in every decision you will make. In fact, it is ultimately an issue about salvation. Either you submit to the loving ownership of Jesus over your life, or you remain a slave to yourself and the sinful impulses of your heart.

part 3: A JEALOUS LORDSHIP

Do you think jealousy is a bad thing? My wife and I met in our mid-twenties, and we had both dated other people. As a matter of fact, when we met, I had just ended a four-year relationship and she had just broken off an engagement. This was a challenge for us both. She wondered if I still had feelings for my ex, and I wondered how big the diamond ring was that she gave back to her ex-fiancé.

Our love for each other generated jealousy. I didn't want her to talk to her ex-fiancé. I didn't even want her to think about him. I wanted all of her affection and attention.

✛ How can jealousy in a relationship be a good thing? When does it become bad?

Read Exodus 20:4-6. What can you learn about God's jealousy from this story? The first one is provided as an example for you to get started.

1) He is jealous of the love you have for anyone or anything else that replaces your love for Him as Lord.

2)

3)

4)

God has the right to be jealous for the affections of His creation. After all, He is the most supreme being in all the universe and therefore deserves that attention. Who or what is receiving the greatest praise in our lives? Are we, in some sense, cheating on God? Are we committing spiritual adultery when we love other parts of creation more than the Creator? When we realize that God is far better than anything else, we echo the words of the apostle Paul when he said, "But everything that was a gain to me, I have considered to be a loss because of Christ. More than that, I also consider everything to be a loss in view of the surpassing value of knowing Christ Jesus my Lord. Because of Him I have suffered the loss of all things and consider them filth, so that I may gain Christ" (Phil. 3:7-8).

part 4: LORDSHIP IS FOUNDATIONAL

+ When it comes to building a house, what are the most important things to get right?

+ Why is the foundation of a house so important? If the foundation isn't secure, how will the rest of the house suffer?

+ **Read Mathew 7:24-27**. Why is it so important that we build our lives on a secure foundation?

The lordship of Christ is the foundation for *The True Love Project*. It's an issue of ownership. Either Jesus is Lord or you are lord. You're not big enough, strong enough, or smart enough to be Lord, but Jesus is.

+ How has this lesson changed your views on sexuality and purity?

session 2: THE COST OF OWNERSHIP

+ Notes on interview with Perry Noble:

CONSIDER THIS

+ What is something you have learned about yourself during this session?

+ How would you respond to someone who said that it is possible to have Jesus as Savior but not as Lord?

+ Why does the issue of lordship affect so many aspects of your life? What does life look like if you are lord? What does life look like if Jesus is Lord?

HIGHLIGHTS

From Clayton's teaching, your personal reflection, and the interview, what impacted you from this session?

+

+

+

ACTION POINTS

+

+

+

session 3:
THE BIBLE ON SEX

Then the LORD God said "It is not good for the man to be alone. I will make a helper as his complement."

GENESIS 2:18

3 session 3: THE BIBLE ON SEX

It comes as no surprise that our culture sends a confusing message regarding sex, romance, and intimacy. Instead of supporting the biblical view that sex is good and is a gift, it promotes the misunderstanding that sex is everything or is nothing at all. However, if we, under the lordship of Christ, are to understand our sexuality in light of God's original design and intention, then we must turn to what the Bible has to say on the subject.

video guide:

SEX IS NOT EVERYTHING:
When sex is everything, the result is sexual _____.

SEX IS NOT NOTHING:
This perspective places sex in a category of _____ and nasty things that make you feel yucky.

For some, sex is completely _____, and the result is sexual confusion.

SEX IS A GIFT:
Sex is a good _____ that is given to us by a good God who intentionally created sex as a means of _____ and procreation.

Sexual intimacy was _____ in the mind of God as a gift to His children.

SEX IS GOOD:
It came from God, and God gives _____ things to His children.

God instigated sex in the institution of _____, even commanding Adam and Eve to come together physically.

For us, sex is a good _____ that is waiting for us in the relationship of marriage.

video feedback:

+ What are some misconceptions regarding sex in culture today?

+ Why do you think the biblical portrait of sex is often overlooked and set aside within our culture?

+ Why would it be unfulfilling to view sex as "everything"?

+ Why would it be unfulfilling to view sex as "nothing"?

+ Why is it important to emphasize that God is the Author of sex and that He created it as a good gift?

+ How can the biblical portrait of sex (as good and as a gift) lead to a life that is both fulfilling and honoring to Christ?

Develop and post a personal tweet or Facebook status related to this session using the hashtag #trueloveproject

part 1: CULTURAL CONFUSION

When sex is everything to you, it becomes the centerpiece of your life. It's the ultimate goal. The big win. The means to satisfy emotional needs. A person who has this perspective may think about it constantly, or perhaps even size-up others as potential sex partners. In short, they can't stop fantasizing about it. For them, sex is an idol, and the result is sexual obsession.

+ What consequences accompany the belief that sex is everything?

+ How does our culture promote the belief that sex is everything?

+ How does believing that sex is everything actually minimize sex? How might that belief leave you feeling unfulfilled?

Another equally destructive perspective places sex in a category of shame. This view sees sex as a nasty or disgusting practice. Those that follow this perspective are offended by the very word *sex*. Why would someone have such a negative perspective? Maybe it brings up unpleasant memories of childhood, an unhealthy relationship, or even an out-of-control party. Perhaps this perspective grew from being sexually abused, manipulated, or raped. For this person, sex is gross, and the result is sexual confusion.

+ What is inaccurate about this perspective of sex?

Can you identify with either of these distorted views? If so, take a few minutes to pray, asking for grace, healing, and a teachable heart to understand sex in the way that God intended.

part 2: BIBLICAL CLARITY

Read Genesis 2:18-25

+ What do these verses communicate about God's original design for:

RELATIONSHIPS?

PHYSICAL INTIMACY?

MARRIAGE?

God uses sexual intimacy between a husband and wife for many purposes, some of which include:

PROCREATION: Sex is the physical act that God uses to populate the earth with people He loves. How is this a gift?

RELATIONAL INTIMACY: Sex allows a married couple to be attentive to their spouse's needs and feelings. How is this a gift?

PHYSICAL INTIMACY: In marriage, the bedroom can become a place of mutual trust, patience, and understanding. How is this a gift?

Sex is essentially an act of communication. It is the physical display of an emotional and spiritual bond. While sex is not the primary means of communicating affections for another, it is the byproduct of loving someone daily and serving him or her faithfully in the marriage relationship.

part 3: UNREAL EXPECTATIONS

Hopefully at this point you are thinking something along the lines of:

I am going to submit myself to Jesus and follow His plan for my life. I realize that giving control to Jesus means also surrendering my sexual desires to His lordship. I am going to live by His expectations, knowing that pursuing physical purity will ultimately bring greater joy in the end.

This is certainly a good start, but it is also important to be on guard against false expectations about what intimacy within marriage will look like.

+ What expectations do you have about sex within marriage?

+ Here are a few unrealistic expectations about sex within marriage:

1) Sex will be hot and passionate every time.
2) Sex will be frequent.
3) Sex will meet all of my intimacy needs.

+ Why do you think these might be unrealistic expectations?

There are a number of reasons that we have unrealistic expectations about sex. Some of which include:

1) American culture is obsessed with sex.
2) Church leaders often give the impression that sex within marriage will satisfy all of your expectations.

+ How have you seen American culture support unrealistic ideas about sex? How have you seen the church support unrealistic ideas about sex?

part 4: GODLY COUNSEL

The key to correcting unrealistic expectations about sex is honesty. This is why it is important to have open and honest discussions with moms, dads, pastors, and leaders about the reality of sex. A lot of good can come from honest and open conversation. For example:

+ Teenagers are less likely to engage in sexual activity if their parents express disapproval.[1]
+ When parents instruct their teenagers about sex through ongoing conversation, the vast majority of those teenagers will rely on their parents, not their friends or the media, for guidance and information about sex.[2]

Given that sex is the union of two bodies and souls within a lifelong covenant of marriage, it is essential to understand the truth and expectations surrounding it.

Read Proverbs 4 and summarize the benefits of pursuing wisdom.

+ Have you ever had a biblical conversation about sex? When and with whom?

+ Who can you turn to for wisdom and counsel? What is preventing you from approaching them to talk about this subject?

+ How has this session challenged your beliefs about sex and intimacy?

---

[1] R.P. Lederman, W. Chan, and C. Roberts-Gray, "Sexual Risk Attitudes and Intentions of Youth Aged 12-14 Years: Survey Comparisons of Parent-Teen Prevention and Control Groups, (Behavioral Medicine 29, no. 4, 2004), 155-163.

[2] C. McNeely, M.L. Shew, T. Beuring, R. Sieving, B.C. Miller, and R.W. Blum, "Mothers' Influence on the Timing of First Sex among 14- and 15-Year-Olds," (Journal of Adolescent Health 31, no. 3, 2002), 251-273.

session 3: THE BIBLE ON SEX

+ Notes on interview with Jud and Lori Wilhite:

CONSIDER THIS

+ How does culture influence our beliefs regarding sex and purity? How do our past experiences influence those beliefs?

+ What did you learn about the Bible's perspective on sex and purity from this session? How did it challenge you?

+ How is the Bible's view of sex within marriage better than culture's view?

HIGHLIGHTS

From Clayton's teaching, your personal reflection, and the interview, what impacted you from this session?

+

+

+

ACTION POINTS

+
+
+

session 4:
YOUR HEART MATTERS

For from within, out of people's hearts, come evil thoughts, sexual immoralities, thefts, murders, adulteries, greed, evil actions, deceit, promiscuity, stinginess, blasphemy, pride, and foolishness. All these evil things come from within and defile a person.

MARK 7:21-23

session 4: YOUR HEART MATTERS

Often absent from discussions about sex and purity are in-depth conversations about why we do the things we do. In other words, when it comes to making decisions about what we do with our bodies, it is important that we understand the role of our hearts in the decision-making process. By understanding the corruption of our hearts, we will be in a better position to see how our hearts function as the command center of our lives. We will also realize our desperate need to have our hearts made new in Christ.

video guide:

COMMAND CENTER OF YOUR LIFE:

When it comes to the biblical understanding of the heart, we need to realize that the heart is more than just the center of our human _____.

The heart is the _____ center of human life. It controls and influences _____ a person does.

DECEITFUL AND CORRUPT:

When we think about our hearts, we assume that they are _____ and filled with _____.

"The heart is more _____ than anything else, and incurable—who can understand it?" Jeremiah 17:9

You need to realize that you really don't have a _____ problem, a sex problem, a pornographic problem, or a _____ problem. What you really have is a _____ problem.

MADE NEW IN CHRIST:

The good news is that the power of the _____ can change our sick, deceitful hearts and make them brand new.

_____ is the cure for your heart problem.

video feedback:

+ Have you ever thought about the central role your heart plays in forming your beliefs about sex and purity? Why or why not?

+ Why would it be important to talk about the role of the heart in making decisions regarding sexual purity? How does this influence the way we view sexual temptation?

+ Given the Bible's portrayal of the human heart, why should we be hesitant to trust it when deciding what to do with our bodies?

+ Why do we need Christ to give us a new heart? How can this provide hope in the fight against sexual temptation?

Develop and post a personal tweet or Facebook status related to this session using the hashtag #trueloveproject

part 1: MORE THAN FEELINGS

✛ List some ways we describe our feelings by using the word *heart*.

1) Example: I love you with all my heart!

2)

3)

4)

5)

We usually think of the heart as the center of human affections. However, the Bible describes it as being much more than that. In fact, the heart actually represents the center of an entire person. It is the command center of one's life, controlling and influencing everything.

✛ What do the following verses communicate about the relationship between the heart and one's behavior?

Then He said, "What comes out of a person—that defiles him. For from within, out of people's hearts, come evil thoughts, sexual immoralities, thefts, murders, adulteries, greed, evil actions, deceit, promiscuity, stinginess, blasphemy, pride, and foolishness. All these evil things come from within and defile a person."
(MARK 7:20-23)

"You have heard that it was said, Do not commit adultery. But I tell you, everyone who looks at a woman to lust for her has already committed adultery with her in his heart."
(MATT. 5:27-28)

For there is no good tree which produces bad fruit, nor, on the other hand, a bad tree which produces good fruit. For each tree is known by its own fruit. For men do not gather figs from thorns, nor do they pick grapes from a briar bush. The good man out of the good treasure of his heart brings forth what is good; and the evil man out of the evil treasure brings forth what is evil; for his mouth speaks from that which fills his heart.
(LUKE 6:43-45)

part 2: HEART CORRUPTION

We often assume our hearts are innocent and filled with love. When it comes to relationships, you've probably heard people say things like, "Just follow your heart" or "trust your heart and go where it leads you."

+ How has the heart been described to you? Has popular advice on the heart ("Just follow your heart") ever influenced your decisions in relationships? Explain.

The Bible describes the heart a little differently:

> *The heart is more deceitful than anything else, and incurable—*
> *who can understand it?*
> (JER. 17:9)

+ Why do you think the Bible describes the heart this way?

+ Given that only Scripture can be fully trusted because it is the Word of God, why do we often treat the heart as the ultimate truth? When has your heart led you down the wrong path?

James understood that all sin and impurity first flows from the heart before it shows up in our actions. He said:

> *What is the source of wars and fights among you? Don't they come from the cravings that are at war within you? You desire and do not have. You murder and covet and cannot obtain. You fight and war. You do not have because you do not ask. You ask and don't receive because you ask with wrong motives, so that you may spend it on your evil desires.*
> (JAS. 4:1-3)

When it comes to the heart, you need to realize that you really don't have a lust problem, a sex problem, a pornographic problem, or even a behavioral problem. Ultimately, you have a heart problem. The human heart is deceitful, sick, and confused. To put it simply, the human heart is sinful.

part 3: HEART FAILURE

We like to think that we are better than other people. We see ourselves as being superior to "sexual perverts" that we read about online or see on the news. But in one sense, every single one of us is a sexual sinner. Before you begin to think that your heart is not that sick, you might want to read something Jesus had to say about the human heart when it comes to sexual sin.

> *"You have heard that it was said, Do not commit adultery. But I tell you, everyone who looks at a woman to lust for her has already committed adultery with her in his heart."*
> (MATT. 5:27-28)

+ How does Jesus overturn any idea of self-righteousness in these verses?

+ Why does Jesus identify sexual sin as something of the heart, not just something physical?

The Jews were accustomed to being led by religious leaders, known as the Pharisees. The Pharisees were focused on outward behavior. Their primary focus was to make sure people kept the law and other man-made rules. The Pharisees believed that enforcing these laws brought them favor with God, but they ignored the place where sin starts—the heart.

+ Do you ever try to earn God's favor? Explain. How can you combat the idea that you have to earn God's approval in your daily life?

Unlike the Pharisees, Jesus is always pointing our attention back inside. He wants us to focus on the engine, not the paint job. He wants us to examine the source of all our desires, and He wants to change that source. God sees the heart. It is there that Christ lives.

part 4: HEART TRANSPLANT

Of course, the fallen heart isn't the end of the story. **Read Ezekiel 36:26-27.** According to these verses, what is the remedy for our heart condition?

Our heart problem sounds like bad news, and it is. But there is good news of hope in your quest for purity and true love.

Romans 6:23 says that even though sin brings death, God offers the gift of eternal life through Jesus Christ. In other words, Jesus is the cure for your heart problem...

> ...and your lust problem.
> ...and your shame problem.
> ...and your guilt problem.
> ...and your porn problem.
> ...and your sex problem.
> ...and your _____ problem.
> ...and your _____ problem.
> ...and your _____ problem.
> ...and your _____ problem.

+ Can you notice a considerable change in the desires and motives of your heart since becoming a Christian? Explain.

+ In what areas of your life do you still struggle with sin? How is Jesus the answer to these problems?

session 4: YOUR HEART MATTERS

+ Notes on interview with Ocielia Gibson:

CONSIDER THIS

+ What have you learned about your own heart from this session?

+ Why is it not enough to focus merely on a change of behavior when dealing with sexual sins? Why must we also focus on a change of heart?

+ Do you consider it good news or bad news that you must rely on the grace of God to change your heart? Explain.

HIGHLIGHTS

From Clayton's teaching, your personal reflection, and the interview, what impacted you from this session?

+

+

+

ACTION POINTS

+
+
+

session 5:
PURITY FROM WITHIN

Yahweh, if You considered sins,
Lord, who could stand?
But with You there is forgiveness,
so that You may be revered.

PSALM 130:3-4

5 session 5: PURITY FROM WITHIN

Many people misunderstand the biblical view of sex and have experienced sexual sin as a result of sinfulness. That being said, it is important to emphasize our need to be forgiven and to forgive. Even if you have compromised on your physical or heart purity in the past, you are never beyond the grace of God's forgiveness. Through Christ, not only can forgiveness be received and extended, but purity can also be restored.

video guide:

When it comes to the topic of forgiveness—from sexual sins or other sins—there are two realities you need to consider:

You may need to _____ God's forgiveness for the mistakes you've made.

You may need to _____ someone for the sins they committed against you.

RECEIVE GOD'S FORGIVENESS:

The first step to this kind of new beginning is to _____ your sin and _____ of your sin.

CONFESS: When we confess our sin to God, we are "_____ up, admitting to and agreeing with" God that we are _____ and sinful.

REPENT: To repent simply means to "turn _____ and turn around."

EXTEND FORGIVENESS TO OTHERS:

Forgiveness is how God _____ us.

Forgiveness is how we _____ ourselves.

video feedback:

+ By realizing that sexual sin can be both physical (sexual activity before marriage, etc.) and of the heart (lust, coveting, etc.), why is it necessary to emphasize our need for forgiveness?

+ In light of the Bible's teaching that we should forgive in the same manner in which we have been forgiven, how should you respond toward those who have sinned against you?

+ Why is it important to emphasize both confession and repentance when it comes to dealing with past sexual sins? What does this look like practically?

+ If you have compromised in your path towards purity, how encouraging is it to hear that Christ is able to make you pure by His grace in your life? Explain.

Develop and post a personal tweet or Facebook status related to this session using the hashtag #trueloveproject

parts 1 & 2: A STORY OF ABUSE AND REDEMPTION

I (Sharie King) was three years old when my mom and dad divorced. I didn't carry any memories of living with my dad because I was so young when they split. That being said, I didn't know what to expect when my mom gave her heart to a new man three years later. Outwardly, he seemed like a dream. He was a financially stable man from a solid family who liked to have a good time with my mom. But underneath the facade was a dark heart that lured him into a perverted relationship with a six-year old girl—me.

From the ages of six to ten, this man acted on his polluted desires. He invaded my body and abused my heart. I did not have a correct understanding of fatherly behavior or a relationship with my real dad. Thus, I was blinded to the fact that this man was a predator. He was always around but never engaging. He would come to a dance recital here and there, but never asked things like, "How was your day at school?" or "Did you enjoy your soccer game?" He wouldn't take my brother and I outside to kick the soccer ball, but he was more than willing to come to my room in the mornings and take me to his bed. He was only interested in me when I was under the covers, behind closed doors. It began with cuddling, but it progressed over the years. Two things showed me how inappropriately he was treating me. First, as a preteen, I began to notice and like boys. The sexual part of me began to come alive. Second, my brother and I accidentally walked in on my mom and step dad in their bedroom one Saturday morning. I saw him doing things with my mom that he made me do with him behind closed doors. The shame was instant and unbearable. I had to keep everything hidden at all costs. I was scared that the person I loved the most in this world, my mom, would feel betrayed by me if she knew. I was afraid she would hate me. I was a terrified fifth grader. I felt different, dirty, and alone. I never invited friends over to my house because of my secret. I had to keep everyone at a distance. If they found out, would I ever be accepted or loved? If they came too close, would they become his victim, too?

During this time, my mom regained an interest in church. Sunday mornings were always tense as my mom and step dad fought over whether we would attend church or go to the lake. Often, my mom's determination won out. I was exposed to church, God's people, and the Bible for the first time. I began to believe the amazing stories I heard in Sunday School, one of which changed my life. My step dad became bolder with his abuse. He stopped coming into my room to get me, and instead, he made me come to him. If I didn't, he'd hover over my bed until I complied. Then I decided I wasn't going to walk to his bedroom anymore. As I predicted, he wasn't going to let me off the hook. One morning, he came to my room and began shaking me aggressively to wake me up. There is no way he thought I was still sleeping, but I refused to take my face out of my pillow. I wasn't sure what would happen next, but in that moment, I remembered a picture of Jesus that I had seen at church. Seeing His face, I cried to God to rescue me like He rescued the Israelites from Egypt. My body felt terrified, hot, and sweaty, but I noticed that my step dad stopped shaking me. I peaked out of the corner of my eye; he was leaving. I had been rescued. The same thing happened again the next morning. He came in and tried to get me to come with him. I buried my head in my pillow and prayed to God. This time he left and never came back. Maybe he was afraid of getting caught. Perhaps the Lord heightened this fear to keep him from me. He had a lot to lose with a computer-engineering career, lake front property, a nice sports car, and a spotless reputation. I don't know why he stopped, but I do know that God answered the prayers of a little girl—a girl who hadn't yet received Jesus as her Savior, but already knew that God was a saver. This is my story. With a past like mine, I wondered if I had anything beautiful to offer my husband. Would the man of my future see me as dirty, tainted, and used? Or would he see the jewel God had rescued?

During this time, I came to realize that sexual sin is paralyzing and embarrassing. However, I also came to realize that God is not paralyzed by our sin. Sin doesn't intimidate God—He already conquered it.

I came to realize that I had to receive God's forgiveness for my own personal sin and extend forgiveness to the one who had sinned against me. I had to choose to forgive the man who victimized me for almost five years. While it wasn't easy, I was able to extend forgiveness because Jesus had first extended it to me.

Jesus wants to forgive us for the sins we've committed with our bodies against ourselves and against others, and He wants us to forgive our offenders, as well. I've had to learn how to do both and am still learning by God's grace.

part 3: PAST MISTAKES AND GRACE

After hearing part of Sharie's story, maybe you are also thinking about whether your future spouse will see you as used or tainted. Maybe your dark stain did not originate with someone else, but it was your own doing. You said yes to a boyfriend before you were ready. Or maybe your physical desires seemed uncontrollable and you convinced your girlfriend to give in. Maybe you didn't go "all the way," but you know what you did was sexually sinful nonetheless. Or perhaps your shame is hidden out of everyone's view in your own mind's fantasy. You haven't been with anyone, but the visions in your head torment you.

It would be a tragedy for you to participate in *The True Love Project* and walk away feeling hopeless because you're not a virgin or because you've messed up. God is willing and able to cleanse, heal, and forgive you. You are not damaged goods, because there is no sin that intimidates God. God's grace is greater than any past mistake. Losing your virginity doesn't disqualify you from joy, peace, pleasure, or love. Jesus can take your biggest mess and make it your greatest message.

+ Since sexual sin is rooted in the heart, why is it important for everyone to rely on God's grace? How does this drive us toward the cross?

+ **Read 1 John 2:1-2.** What hope do we have after we have sinned?

+ How does it make you feel to know that Jesus will be righteous and holy for you when you cannot be righteous and holy on your own?

+ How does knowing that Jesus will never abandon you encourage you to pursue purity?

part 4: YOUR STORY OF FORGIVENESS

+ If your past mistakes include the loss of your virginity, how should you respond to this message?

+ Consider writing out your own personal story to God.
  Include the following elements:
      1) Receiving God's forgiveness
      2) Extending forgiveness to others

session 5: PURITY FROM WITHIN

+ Notes on interview with Marian Jordan Ellis:

CONSIDER THIS

+ What have you learned about God's forgiveness from this session?

+ How does knowing that our purity comes from Jesus help us in our fight for sexual purity? Why is it important to emphasize this point when we fall into sexual sin?

+ How does knowing our true identity in Christ influence us positively when making decisions about our purity?

HIGHLIGHTS

From Clayton's teaching, your personal reflection, and the interview, what impacted you from this session?

+

+

+

ACTION POINTS

+
+
+

6

session 6:
OUR FINAL DESTINATION

"My purity is for His delight primarily. If I am still single at age 70, my heart will be full of joy over the relationship I have shared with my regal King, thankful that immorality never harmed the depth of intimacy we have shared. As my King Regent, He has every right to all of me — including the sexual me. I am His alone. He is the main thing, the only thing that matters ultimately. I am waiting for unimaginable closeness with Him forever. And I want nothing on earth that impinges on my delight in Him forever."

**-DR. RICHARD ROSS,
CO-FOUNDER OF *TRUE LOVE WAITS***

session 6: OUR FINAL DESTINATION

After having spent five sessions laying the biblical groundwork for God's view concerning Himself, ourselves, sex, and purity, we now turn our attention to practical ways these beliefs work themselves out in everyday life. In this session, we will focus not only on the end goal of our sexual purity, but also the end goal for all of our lives—Jesus.

video guide:

WHERE YOU ARE GOING:

It's not your _____ that gets you to your destination. It's taking _____ by heading in the right direction.

Before you can strike out in the right _____, you must decide where it is you want to go.

The end goal is not to be a _____ on your wedding day. The end goal is to be found _____ on judgment day.

Jesus is the _____.

HOW YOU GET THERE:

+ **SUBMISSION:**

+ **DIRECTION:**

+ **INSTRUCTION:**

+ **ACTION:**

+ **DESTINATION:**

video feedback:

+ How would you explain the relationship between destination and directions? How does the former determine the latter?

+ Though staying a virgin before marriage is important and something that should be fought for, why should Jesus, and not virginity, be our end goal?

+ What practical steps can you take to honor and glorify Jesus through your sexuality?

+ What stood out to you in this session? Why? How do these ideas cause you to reconsider your direction in your path toward purity?

Develop and post a personal tweet or Facebook status related to this session using the hashtag #trueloveproject

part 1: HOW ARE YOU GETTING THERE?

We have discovered that sexual desire is both good and a gift, but even if your intentions are good, you must be moving in the right direction to arrive at the correct destination. All of us are heading in a certain direction whether we are aware of it or not.

+ At this point in your life, where are you heading sexually? How did you get on this path?

It's not your intention that gets you to your destination; it's taking action by heading in the right direction. How has taking action, not just having good intention, played a major role in getting you to a certain goal in school? in your sport? in your relationships?

+ How does destination influence the directions?

What is your desired destination when it comes to sex and romance? Are you heading in the right direction to make it to that destination? Explain.

part 2: WHERE ARE YOU GOING?

What is your ultimate destination? Is your goal to remain pure until your wedding night? Is it to have really great sex in the future? Are you living for the wedding day itself? Do you only dream about the wedding dress or the honeymoon night?

While there's certainly no harm in imagining those special moments, they should never be the primary motivation for marrying another person. Marriage, though good and a gift from God, is not eternal. If you idolize marriage and make it your sole pursuit in life, you will worship the myth of a "perfect marriage" or a "perfect mate" and be crushed when you find out that neither exists.

✛ Do you think that everything will "fall into place" once you find the right person to marry? Why or why not? What is wrong with this belief?

Of course, this does not mean that you shouldn't pursue virginity—you absolutely should pursue virginity. However, virginity should not be the primary goal of your life. Why? Because virginity isn't your ultimate destination. The only goal worth whole-heartedly pursuing is to know Jesus, and your ultimate destination should be the kingdom of God. As you pick your destination, realize that Jesus is better than a good marriage, great sex, or even being able to say that you were a virgin on your honeymoon. For Christians, the goal is not to be a virgin on your wedding day; the goal is to be found faithful to Jesus on judgment day. How can pursuing virginity as the ultimate goal create idols within your heart?

✛ Why can't virginity be the ultimate goal? Why is it too small of a pursuit?

✛ How will making Jesus the ultimate goal and destination of your life drive you toward sexual purity? Why is this goal supreme?

part 3: THE NAVIGATIONAL TOOL

Now that we know our destination, how do we get there? Consider what the psalmist said:

Your word is a lamp for my feet and a light on my path. I have solemnly sworn to keep your righteous judgments.
(PS. 119:105-106)

My life is constantly in danger, yet I do not forget Your instruction. The wicked have set a trap for me, but I have not wandered from Your precepts. I have Your decrees as a heritage forever; indeed, they are the joy of my heart. I am resolved to obey your statutes to the very end.
(PS. 119:109-112)

+ According to these verses, who should we look to for directions?

+ What method did the psalmist use to stay focused on the right direction?

+ Are there other ways to get to your destination besides fixing your eyes on His Word? Why is this the only way?

+ How have you been trying to stay focused on the right direction in your own life? Why is sheer willpower alone not enough to pursue Christ in purity?

part 4: HEADING TO YOUR COORDINATES

Consider the importance of His Word when trying to move in the right direction...

> *How can a young man keep his way pure? By keeping Your word.* (PS. 119:9)

✝ What is the connection the writer makes between God's Word and a life of purity?

> *I have treasured Your word in my heart so that I might not sin against You.* (PS. 119:11)

✝ How can opening your heart up to the wisdom and direction of Scripture displace sin in your life?

> *Your decrees are my delight and my counselors.* (PS. 119:24)

✝ How can God's Word give you wisdom in every relationship?

> *Help me stay on the path of Your commands, for I take pleasure in it. Turn my heart to Your decrees and not to material gain. Turn my eyes from looking at what is worthless; give me life in Your ways.*
> (PS. 119:35-37)

When I'm confused about who to date or marry, direct me in the path of Your commands. When my heart wants something that I shouldn't pursue, turn my heart toward Your statutes and not toward selfish gain. When I'm struggling with lust or tempted to look at porn, turn my eyes from worthless things.

There is a pattern and a rhythm to following Jesus as His disciple, and it begins with being filled with His promises. By clinging to the Word, not only do Christians grow in their faith and love for God, but they also receive clearer directions to make it to their ultimate destination—Jesus.

session 6: OUR FINAL DESTINATION

+ Notes on interview with Jeff Bethke:

CONSIDER THIS

+ How could the pursuit of virginity become an idol in your heart? Why is it important to emphasize the pursuit of Jesus through sexual purity?

+ Why is it important that we fight against the fleeting pleasures of sin by emphasizing the infinite pleasures found in Christ?

+ Why is it important to be surrounded by Christian community in your personal fight for purity? How can you help serve your Christian brothers and sisters in their journey?

HIGHLIGHTS

From Clayton's teaching, your personal reflection, and the interview, what impacted you from this session?

+

+

+

ACTION POINTS

+
+
+

7

session 7:
HATE IT, STARVE IT, OUTSMART IT

You will never win the battle with sin by just trying harder. Effort alone is not enough. Sin is stronger and more experienced than you, and like a serial killer it will not settle for anything other than the complete taking of your life. If you want to defeat sin and temptation, you have to have a better plan, one capable of a multi-faceted attack.

-CLAYTON KING

7

session 7: HATE IT, STARVE IT, OUTSMART IT

Once we have decided on our final arriving point—Jesus—and have moved in the direction of pursuing Him, it is important for us to develop and maintain a plan of action to help us reach our goal. This plan of action is not an attempt to create artificial rules or standards that we live by in order to feel self-righteous. Instead, it is a biblical response to the grace of God working through our lives. In this session, we are going to explore some proactive ways to fight sexual temptation and cultivate genuine desire for purity and holiness.

video guide:

We are to be pro-active when it comes to _____ remaining sin in our lives, and one of the ways to do so is to have a biblical plan of attack.

HATE IT:

STARVE IT:

OUTSMART IT:

You will need to _____ this battle plan and _____ it to your certain situation.

You are not fighting _____ victory; you are fighting _____ victory.

video feedback:

+ Why is it important to have a biblical plan of action when it comes to fighting against sin in your life?

+ What do you think about the psalmist's battle plan? How could you adopt and adapt it to your personal struggles?

+ Explain why having a plan isn't an attempt to earn grace but rather a natural response to grace.

+ What additional things can you do to help guard you on the path toward Christ?

Develop and post a personal tweet or Facebook status related to this session using the hashtag #trueloveproject

part 1: CHRISTIAN ARSENAL

When it comes to fighting for sexual purity, it is important to remember that our strength is not in human effort. Rather, our strength is in the power of the Holy Spirit working through our lives as we submit to the lordship of Christ.

✝ **Read Ephesians 3:14-16.** What did Paul pray for his brothers and sisters in Ephesus? What can we learn from his prayer about finding strength to fight the battle against sin?

It is crucial that every Christian understands one simple truth in our battle for holiness: When it comes to sexual sin, the battle has already been fought and the victory has already been won. You are not fighting FOR victory; you are fighting FROM victory.

✝ Why is it important to emphasize that we are fighting from victory instead of for victory? Of the two, which emphasizes grace and Christ's victory over sin and death? Which emphasizes human effort? Explain.

✝ When Christians say that holiness is both a position and a pursuit, what exactly do they mean?

The fight against sexual sin is won when you trust that Jesus has something better for you than the momentary pleasures of sexual sin. As John Piper says, "The fire of lust's pleasures must be fought with the fire of God's pleasures."[1]

✝ Sin is deceitful. It tells us it will provide ultimate satisfaction, but it always fails in the end. How can we use this knowledge in the fight against sin?

[1] John Piper, *Future Grace* (Colorado Springs, Colorado: Multnomah Books, 2012), 336.

part 2: THE BATTLE PLAN

Even though we approach our fight for purity from a position of victory, it is important to have a battle plan to help us along the way. It is good for us to have a plan that stands on the victory of Christ over sin.

> *How I love Your instruction! It is my meditation all day long. Your commands make me wiser than my enemies, for they are always with me. I have more insight than all my teachers because Your decrees are my meditation. I understand more than the elders because I obey Your precepts. I have kept my feet from every evil path to follow Your word. I have not turned from Your judgments, for You Yourself have instructed me. How sweet Your word is to my taste—sweeter than honey in my mouth. I gain understanding from Your precepts; therefore I hate every false way.*
>
> (Ps. 119:97-104)

✝ What does the writer mean when he says he hates "every false way"? Are we supposed to hate sin? Why?

✝ How does the writer starve sin by keeping his feet "from every evil path"? How can we apply this to our own lives when dealing with sexual sin?

✝ How does the writer plan on outsmarting his enemy? What must he turn to in order to do this?

We must adopt this battle plan to our particular struggles. But remember, despite whatever your personal struggle may be, Jesus has given you victory over sin. You are simply learning to live out that victory by waging war against temptation through daily reliance upon the Holy Spirit.

part 3: REAL-TIME WARFARE

How can you adapt the battle plan to your situation? Here are some recommendations...

+ Ask someone to hold you accountable in what you watch on the TV and Internet.

+ Sign up with a few friends for an online filtering service. This program records every accessed website, then sends out a list of those websites in an email once a week.

+ Perform regular "heart checks" to evaluate what you've been placing your hope and identity in lately.

+ Delete certain contacts in your phone or on your Facebook account that might be a temptation for you.

+ Ask an accountability partner or parent to put safeguards on your phone that prevent you from accessing certain sites.

+ Ask yourself the following: Is my hope and security found in my present relationship with Jesus, or in the hopeful relationship with a guy/girl?

+ Avoid looking at the magazine rack at the checkout counter if it causes you to stumble.

+ Don't read certain romance novels that easily lead to sexual fantasizing or distort the biblical picture of romance.

+ Pay attention to the ebb and flow of your schedule, knowing that temptation usually strikes at certain times of the day or when having feelings of fatigue, loneliness, etc.

+ Seek accountability to help you guard your heart against going too far emotionally in a relationship.

In essence, adapting the plan to your situation means first recognizing where your weaknesses lie. By being aware of areas that trigger sexual temptation and sin, you can be in a better position when it comes to battling for personal purity.

part 4: TIME TO FIGHT

+ Why is it important to think about your specific weaknesses when developing a strategy to fight sin in your life?

The fight against sexual sin doesn't include a "one size fits all" strategy.
Use the space below to map out your personal battle plan in your pursuit of purity.

session 7: HATE IT, STARVE IT, OUTSMART IT

+ Notes on interview with Steven and Holly Furtick:

CONSIDER THIS

+ What have you learned about your own battle plan when it comes to pursuing sexual purity?

+ How do daily habits influence our decisions regarding sex and purity?

+ Why is it important to implement new habits in your daily life? How can this be done?

HIGHLIGHTS

From Clayton's teaching, your personal reflection, and the interview, what impacted you from this session?

+

+

+

ACTION POINTS

+
+
+

session 8:
SEX, GOD'S GLORY, & YOUR MISSION

When Jesus is Lord of your life, He is Lord of all of your life, including your physical and emotional desires for romance, love, and sex. When you are committed to living a holy life that is set apart for Him, you live a life of worship to Christ and a life of witness to the world.

Our actions communicate what we really believe to both ourselves and others. In the case of sexuality, it is easy to see that what we do with our bodies actually communicates whether we agree with God on the subject or not. Those actions also communicate a positive witness of the gospel to those who are watching. In the end, we need to realize that sex and purity aren't just about sex and purity—they are ultimately about God, His Glory, and our mission here on earth.

video guide:

God didn't save you so you could _____. He saved you so you could serve.

He didn't save you to wait around. He saved you to work and _____.

Our worship is our _____ to the world.

It is an act of worship to stand against the tide of _____ and temptation and to declare, "Jesus is Lord and I belong to Him. I will do what He says."

I'm not promising you that people will _____ your commitment to purity or applaud your battle for holiness.

You represent the _____ of God and you carry the gospel of Jesus Christ with you everywhere you go.

So remember, the _____ impacts your purity, and your purity says something to the world about your commitment to the _____.

video feedback:

+ Summarize Clayton's connection between sex, worship, and witness. Why is it important to think of this topic in such a way?

+ How has Clayton's personal story of standing up and speaking encouraged you to do the same?

+ If you haven't been the greatest witness for Christ in this area of your life, how has this study encouraged you to change?

+ How has this study encouraged you to live for Christ in the area of your sexuality? What will you do differently from this point forward?

Develop and post a personal tweet or Facebook status related to this session using the hashtag #trueloveproject

part 1: LIVING SACRIFICES

When Jesus is Lord of your life, He is Lord of all of your life—including your physical and emotional desires for romance, love, and sex. When you give Him control, you are committing to a holy life that is set apart for Christ. This is an act of worship to God and a witness to the world. When you realize that your body belongs to the Lord, it should cause you to re-think how you live, what you watch, how you act, and even how you think.

+ Read **Romans 12:1-3**. Why is it an act of worship to "present your bodies as a living sacrifice"?

+ What are you communicating to others when you decide to choose God over your own selfish desires?

It is an act of worship and a witness to others when you stand against the tide of sexual sin and declare, "Jesus is Lord and I belong to Him. I will do what He says."

+ Have you ever thought about how your sexual purity reflects the glory of God throughout your life? Why is this an important connection to make?

+ Have you ever considered the fact that your sexual purity affects the mission God has placed on your life? Why is this important? How can you point others to Jesus by pursuing Him in a life of purity?

+ How are you making much of Christ through your life? through your sexual purity? Explain.

part 2: ON MISSION

When all of life is worship, then all aspects of life are lived as being on mission. Whether you consider yourself a missionary or not, the fact remains that if you are a follower of Christ, you are on a mission to make Him known.

The Bible uses a lot of ways to describe what it means to be on mission. Read the following verses and note the different titles and ways Christians are supposed to live.

+ **ACTS 1:18**

+ **2 CORINTHIANS 5:17**

+ **MATTHEW 5:13-16**

+ How is your commitment to purity related to you being a "witness," "ambassador," and "salt and light" to the world?

+ How could our desire to be sexually pure affect our witness? If we chose a life of impurity, how would that affect our witness?

Far too often, people think that the choices they make in regards to sex are unrelated to their Christian life. They have convinced themselves that life is compartmentalized and that certain areas never overlap. However, nothing could be further from the truth. As we have seen, when someone comes to Christ, they recognize that He is not only Savior, but is also Lord of all. And when He saves someone, He saves every part of that person. No part goes unredeemed; every part gets remade. God does this because He designed all things for His glory. And this means that all things, including our sexuality, are capable of reflecting His glory as originally intended.

part 3: WHERE TO GO FROM HERE

If you were created to make much of Christ in every area of your life, including your purity, then how are you measuring up? If your witness for Christ has suffered because of unrepentant sexual sin, take time to confess your shortcomings to God, ask for forgiveness, and repent of your sins. Consider writing out your prayer below.

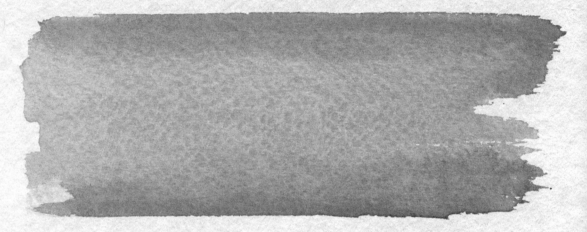

Use the space below to summarize what you have learned throughout this study. What do you hope to remember?

part 4: REPENTANCE

PRAY
+ Establish your dependence on God by praying for the Holy Spirit's help in this process.

IDENTIFY THE SIN
+ Define its practice.
+ Define your heart's motive for the sin.
+ Define the lie—the false belief—that created this motive and its acts.

EMBRACE THE GOSPEL
+ Consider how your sin offends God.
+ Think on the fact that God sent Jesus to die in your place to overcome the offense this sin created.
+ Pray and admit your sin to God. Ask for forgiveness on the basis of Jesus' death on your behalf.

TAKE STEPS TO STOP
+ Memorize Bible verses that relate to your sin, its consequences, and your forgiveness in Christ.
+ Change your thinking.
+ Change behaviors that increase temptation.
+ Change the places you go.
+ Change the people you interact with.
+ Change the things you look at.
+ Change the words you say.
+ Confess your sin to those you've offended and seek their forgiveness.

REPLACE YOUR SIN WITH RIGHTEOUSNESS
+ If you're a Christian, you are joined to Jesus Christ, and His Spirit dwells in you. You can think and act as He does.

SEEK ACCOUNTABILITY IN YOUR LIFE
+ If you haven't already, inform godly friends or a pastor of your sin.
+ Ask for their advice regarding the plan you have adopted and adapted.
+ Make yourself accountable to walk along the specific path you've committed to.[1]

---

[1] Joshua Harris, *Not Even a Hint* (Oregon: Multnomah, 2003), 173-175.

session 8: SEX, GOD'S GLORY, AND YOUR MISSION

+ Notes on interview with Derwin and Vicky Gray:

CONSIDER THIS

+ What is the connection between the way we treat our bodies and God's glory?

+ What is the connection between the way we treat our bodies and our witness for Christ?

+ How has this study on sex and purity impacted your life? How will you treat others differently as a result?

HIGHLIGHTS

From Clayton's teaching, your personal reflection, and the interview, what impacted you from this session?

+

+

+

ACTION POINTS

+
+
+

By the time you have reached this section, you have hopefully gone through all eight sessions of the *True Love Project*. It is our hope and prayer that by this point, the words on this commitment card are an accurate reflection of where your heart is right now in regards to your commitment to Christ in the pursuit of purity. We hope that by this time you have realized that the battle for purity is a lifelong commitment, fought in the grace and strength that God supplies. However, it also a battle that has already been won on our behalf since it is the gospel that defines our purity. By signing this card, you are externally confirming this internal commitment.

True Love Waits Commitment

In light of who God is, what Christ has done for me, and who I am in Him, from this day forward I commit myself to Him in the lifelong pursuit of purity. By His grace, I will continually present myself to Him as a living sacrifice, holy and pleasing to God.

SIGNATURE _____

DATE _____

true love waits.